# WE ARE ONE

# WE ARE ONE

# A 31-DAY MARRIAGE DEVOTION

RICK THOMAS

WE ARE ONE:
A 31-Day Marriage Program

ISBN 978-1-966741-08-4

Rick Thomas

Edited by Sheron Wallace

Life Over Coffee
8595 Pelham Rd Ste 400 #406,
Greenville, SC 29615
LifeOverCoffee.com

Ephesians 5:25-33

Husbands, love your wives, as Christ loved the church and gave himself up for her, that he might sanctify her, having cleansed her by the washing of water with the word, so that he might present the church to himself in splendor, without spot or wrinkle or any such thing, that she might be holy and without blemish. In the same way husbands should love their wives as their own bodies. He who loves his wife loves himself. For no one ever hated his own flesh, but nourishes and cherishes it, just as Christ does the church, because we are members of his body. "Therefore a man shall leave his father and mother and hold fast to his wife, and the two shall become one flesh." This mystery is profound, and I am saying that it refers to Christ and the church. However, let each one of you love his wife as himself, and let the wife see that she respects her husband.

For additional resources, visit
lifeovercoffee.com

# Table of Contents

# Introduction

Welcome to "We Are One—A 31-Day Marriage Devotion." This book is for couples who want to enrich their marriages. I developed this devotional series so that spouses can read one devotional each day for 31 days. But to make the most of this marriage journey, it would be better if you slowed your pace so you have time to reflect, discuss, and apply the material to your life and marriage adequately. Each devotion is the equivalent of a homework assignment that needs time for thorough application. At the end of each short devotion is a section for you to contemplate the questions provided, plus a practical suggestion for you to implement into your marriage.

Transformation is rarely like flipping a switch and moving on to the next thing. Interrelationship challenges and opportunities are reciprocal, give-and-take moments where conversations ensue and continue over days and weeks. If the hurt is deep or the offense is heavy, you may need time to change completely. These devotionals are short sprints, but your marriage is a marathon. Be deliberate, well-paced, and consistent. *We Are One—A 31-Day Marriage Devotion* is a toolbox that will help you change while enhancing your marriage. As you peruse these short chapters, perhaps the Spirit of God will highlight one over the other. There may be a particular need you should address today. Start at the best place for you rather than at the beginning.

Maybe you're not married but hope to be soon. This devotional is the perfect premarriage book. What better time to work on your future marriage and the inevitable problems than before you have them? Remember your small group friendships, too. Doing this devotion in the context of friends adds the benefit of courageous and compassionate accountability.

Rick

# 1

# We Are One

> Therefore a man shall leave his father and his mother and hold fast to his wife, and they shall become one flesh. And the man and his wife were both naked and were not ashamed.
>
> (Genesis 2:24-25)

One of the more common complaints I hear from spouses is when one of the partners in the marriage talks about being alone in their marriage. These lonely spouses perceive a seemingly invisible barrier between each other. It's a communication breakdown, and the reason they cannot change is because the deepest and most intimate component of marriage communication is uniquely spiritual. While couples can relate in many ways, there is one way that is non-negotiable if you intend to engage each other like Christ and His church (Ephesians 5:25-33). That spiritual component is an intimate three-person dynamic between the husband, wife, and God. I'm not necessarily talking about praying together, going to church, reading the Bible, or doing other churchy things— all vital aspects of a sound relationship. I'm speaking of in-depth and comprehensive spiritual communication. Some spouses respond to this spiritual disconnect by saying,

*We talk about God, pray together, and go to church. Our kids are involved in the church's ministries, and we are active churchgoers. I attend the weekly men's meeting, and my wife leads her Bible study. It's not that we don't love God or each other.*

What I'm talking about is not necessarily what a couple or family is doing in their church building with their church friends. Some of the busiest Christians can be some of the most discontented people in their marriages. The biblical term for what is lacking in this kind of marriage is koinonia, from which we get our words communication, community, participation, or fellowship. Koinonia is a three-person construct that represents the deepest possible intimacy a man and woman can experience in their marriage. True koinonia can only happen in your marriage when you share your full experience with God—the good and the bad of it—with your spouse, and your spouse shares their full experience of God with you. That is the highest level of biblical community. It is a free-flowing, dynamic relationship without barriers, interruptions, or hindrances. Koinonia will not happen if either spouse is unwilling to be transparent, honest, open, mature, humble, vulnerable, and intentional with each other. If those character qualities are not present, there is no way for spouses to enjoy true oneness. Three of the more common hindrances to this kind of communication are fear, anger, and unforgiveness. These are koinonia killers.

- Is there fear or inhibition between you and your spouse?
- Do you harbor frustration, impatience, or other forms of anger toward your spouse?
- Are you holding on to unforgiveness because of something your spouse has done in the past?

## Time to Reflect

If you hope to avoid being alone in your marriage, you must work through these communication killers. Identify what is hindering you from having this kind of relationship with your spouse. Consider the three hindrances I suggested or identify other sources for what's impeding your biblical koinonia. Begin a process of change so you can successfully remove anything disrupting your conjugal community.

## Practical Suggestion

Ask the Lord to give you time, context, and courage to discuss these questions with your spouse. The questions below are your koinonia starter pack—sample questions you can ask your spouse to build koinonia. You may add more questions to this list. Plan a few uninterrupted date nights where you can talk. No dinner and a movie; just you and your spouse, eye-to-eye, communicating.

1. Will you help me in this [name a specific area of temptation] in my life?
2. What is God doing in your life—the good and not-so-good?
3. What specific areas are you still struggling with?
4. What have you lately read or heard that is helping you in your sanctification?
5. How can I serve you in a [name a specific area of sanctification] in your life?
6. What has God taught you recently? How have you applied it to your life?

# 2

# Most Important Thing

> So, whether you eat or drink, or whatever you do, do
> all to the glory of God.
>
> (1 Corinthians 10:31)

What is the most important quality you would like to have in your marriage? Of all the qualities to choose from, there is one transcending quality that must be at the top of your list. That one transcending quality is God's glory. If your desire to glorify God is the chief aim of your life and marriage, there is a fantastic chance you will experience a meaningful and satisfying relationship with your spouse, even should your spouse not meet all of your expectations. There is nothing that transcends this God-centered quality in His image bearers. Suppose your chief aim in life is to spread the fame of God—another way of talking about glorifying God. In that case, you can be comforted by the fact that even sin and non-sinful disappointments and letdowns will not overcome your dogged and steadfast determination to be like Jesus—a primary way to glorify God (Ephesians 5:1; 1 Corinthians 11:1). Whenever sin makes its advances, your determination to glorify God will win the war against sin's intent. When the guardian of your heart is the glory of the Lord, you're in the best place to be a good friend, a great lover, and a wonderful spouse. There are many tools available to help you more effectively glorify God. May I share three of them with you?

**PASSION:** Everyone is passionate about something, and that something—whatever it may be—defines them. Nobody lacks emotion. If you look long enough, you will recognize what makes a person emote. Perhaps it's a desire to have a great job, rear spiritual children, or build a secure future—all good things. When it comes to living an effective Christian life, there must be a preeminent longing for His glory that is so high that all other loves look like hate by comparison (Luke 14:26-27).

**REPENTANCE:** Nobody has been able to pull off perfection but Jesus. Your lack of perfect sanctification means you and your spouse are imperfect sinners, even on your best days. Your spouse has sinned against you and God, and you have done similarly. You do not have to be discouraged by this reality if your chief aim is to glorify God. Glorifying God does not imply perfection. Living a perfect life is contrary to the Bible—for all have sinned (Romans 3:23)—and if anyone says they don't sin, they are liars (1 John 1:7-10). But do not fear; there is good news. A person whose primary goal is to glorify God has a great backup plan because that person is a repenting individual. Though you will have lapses in judgment, as experienced by doing something unkind to your spouse, you will respond promptly with a broken-hearted confession (Psalm 51:17) and a request for forgiveness.

**COMMUNITY:** A God-impassioned, repenting person will seek similar companions because kind gravitates to kind. Let me state it another way: regardless of who you are, you will find your kind. The question then becomes, "What kind of people are you pursuing?" The Lord wired you with a herd mentality, which is why humans seek community. We reflect the image of the original community: Father, Son, and Spirit (Genesis 1:26-27). You can discern an individual by assessing their associations—the things they try to fill their lives with, whether it's humans, media, or habits. Nobody intentionally surrounds themselves with things they do not like unless it's unavoidable, e.g., your job.

## Time to Reflect

1.  Does your desire to glorify God give you the wisdom and perseverance to spread the fame of God even when your marriage is not meeting your expectations? Please explain.
2.  How can you more effectively glorify God in your marriage, especially when things do not go your way?

## Practical Suggestion

Rank the three tools I mentioned that help you glorify God—passion, repentance, and community. Which of those three do you need more help with in further development? Find a mentor (preferably your spouse) to create a plan to change what you need to change so you can more effectively spread God's fame in your life and marriage. What does your spouse say about how your passion, repentance, and friends glorify God?

# 3

# His and Her Problems

> Therefore a man shall leave his father and his mother and hold fast to his wife, and they shall become one flesh.
>
> (Genesis 2:24)

I watched my wife go through three miscarriages. They happened to her. It was her pain, her disappointment, her fear, but they were my miscarriages, too. I did not feel hurt the way she did. I have no idea of the physical, mental, and emotional agony of a miscarriage—at least not the way she does. But I hurt because she was hurting. I hurt because I lost something, too. We are one flesh. When someone murdered my brother in 1997, my wife hurt along with me. She did not hurt the way I did, but she hurt because her husband was hurting. We are not two people, acting independently of each other. We are one body (Hebrews 13:3). When I sin—no matter what it is—my wife has a responsibility for that sin. She would never say, "That's Rick's problem. That's his sin." No, it's our sin. She is not guilty of my sin, she does not repent of my sin, and God does not consider her guilty of my sin, but she has a role to play because she is me, and I am her—we are one.

When I sin, she runs to my aid by calling me out and bringing corrective care. She becomes my discipler—my mentor. Similar to when a briar cuts an arm, the body comes to the rescue. Too often when one marriage partner sins, the other spouse acts as though they are not part of the one flesh union. This kind of marriage detachment is Job's wife syndrome: the non-sinning spouse gets mad when the other spouse is in trouble (Job 2:9). Ironically, this means both of them are sinning. When two people respond sinfully to sin, they both are guilty before God and before each other, regardless of who was first to fall. They both need to repent. It's like cursing your arm when it gets cut. That's weird; it's your body. You shouldn't get mad at yourself when something happens to you. Are you following my logic?

It is biblical insanity to get mad at your spouse when they sin. When part of the body rejects another part of the body, you have a schism in the body. You must call a doctor, or, in this case, if you're unwilling to repent, you better call your pastor or some other competent helper. Your one flesh union needs help. Are you a rescuer and restorer or are you a critic and condemner? You'll never be more tested on this than when your spouse does something that annoys you. It may be helpful to remember that your spouse is an instrument the Lord uses to mature you. God will use sin sinlessly to transform His children. We see this in Paul's warning about a person in sin and a person who helps that soul in sin. Take a look at these three verses and note how much time Paul spent talking to the helper (47 words) rather than the person in sin (7 words).

*Brothers, if anyone is caught in any transgression, you who are spiritual should restore him in a spirit of gentleness. Keep watch on yourself, lest you too be tempted. Bear one another's burdens, and*

> so fulfill the law of Christ. For if anyone thinks
> he is something, when he is nothing, he deceives
> himself.
>
> (Galatians 6:1-3)

If you don't see your spouse's problem as your problem, you won't be an active part of the solution, and your marriage will go to places where it cannot recover. Paul warned the restorers to guard their hearts against this kind of self-deception.

## Time to Reflect

1. How would you characterize yourself as it pertains to your spouse: are you more of a restorer or condemner?
2. Do you see your spouse's problems as your problems, too? Please explain.

## Practical Suggestion

Write down one area in which your spouse is weak and how you provide the strength needed to compensate for their weakness. Name one area where you are weak and your spouse complements you with their strength.

# 4

# You Need
# Someone

Then the LORD God said, "It is not good that the
man should be alone; I will make him a helper fit
for him."

(Genesis 2:18)

The difference in how you read this verse depends
on whether you are looking through a dirty or clean
presuppositional window. If you are interpreting Adam's
situation through the lens of your depravity, it would be
easy to conclude that Adam was sinfully lacking and longing
for more than what he had. Suppose you are interpreting
Adam's situation through the presuppositional lens of
contentment, which was his state prior to the fall. In that
case, your understanding of why the Lord said it was not
good for him to be alone will be different. The tendency
is to look at Genesis 2:18 from our fallen experience of
loneliness and needs, which can tempt us to upload the
text from a sin-centered, dirty window perspective. Thus,
we will look back at the text while mapping our fallen
experience over it. Adam was not in sin at the time of this
text. His thoughts and feelings were remarkably different
from how we experience life.

It had not occurred to Adam that there was a problem with not having a wife since no such thing existed at that time. The cliche "you can't know what you can't know" has an important application. It reminds me of a newly hatched duck that sees a dog before anything else. What does it do? It follows the dog, which becomes the duck's parent. A duck does not know what you know, so it follows the dog. Adam was living large. He was benefiting from all the Lord created. To speculate that Adam sinfully longed for something that did not exist would be pushing the text too far. Adam was the hatched duckling. His life was awesome, but the Lord was in creative mode. He knew what needed to happen, and Adam was not part of the decision-making committee (Genesis 1:26-27). Adam's role was to be the happy recipient of whatever the Lord decided to bring his way.

What Adam lacked was not someone to fill his empty love cup but someone who would allow him to display God in the world in a fuller and more robust way. Adam was like the world's greatest baseball player, with no place to play. He was suited up and equipped but had no construct or companion to do the one thing he was designed to do, which was to image the divine community of Father, Son, and Spirit. Adam did not need love but needed someone to receive his love. When Jesus talked about relationships, He did not talk about what we needed from them but what we needed to do for them. For example, when Christ talked about how to live out the Bible well, He said to love the Lord and others were the two greatest commandments (Matthew 22:36-40). The primary direction of God's love is always toward others, not toward ourselves (John 3:16). We give what we possess. We love God and others as we love ourselves.

When Paul talked about a man's relationship with his wife, He said that he should give his life for her (Ephesians 5:25). When Paul gave his version of the two great commandments, he stated that we should count others as more significant than ourselves (Philippians 2:3-4). In a God-centered world, our thoughts are always directed to God and others, just as we love ourselves, which is critical insight when we think about Adam's world. He did not need Eve as though there was something sinfully wrong with him. He needed Eve so he could more effectively image the community that created him. Eve did not need Adam's love because there was nothing sinfully wrong with her. She needed Adam so she could have the opportunity to put the Trinity on display, similar to her husband.

## Time to Reflect

What is the main reason you want your spouse: to meet your desires or to spread the fame of God by imitating the Trinity, which you can do by modeling the mantra—it's more blessed to give than to receive? Please explain your answer.

## Practical Suggestion

In the context of this devotion, you must ensure the direction of your love goes from you and not toward you. What do you need to change about yourself to position your marriage to more effectively spread God's fame?

# 5

# Dating to Divorce

*If we say we have no sin, we deceive ourselves, and the truth is not in us. If we confess our sins, he is faithful and just to forgive us our sins and to cleanse us from all unrighteousness. If we say we have not sinned, we make him a liar, and his word is not in us.*

(1 John 1:8-10)

If you put two sinners in a box, a room, or a home for an extended period with no plan for escape, you can expect problems. There may be a lot of love along the way, but there will also be unavoidable disappointments, arguments, and conflict. The dating couple can break up and go on to the next relationship. Vocational workmates are similar. If you don't like your boss or the environment in which you work, you can move on to the next big thing. Marriage is different. Though it's easy to get into, there is no escape plan other than death. Sadly, too many couples ignore the hardness of their hearts and create an alternate plan: divorce (Matthew 19:8). By the time two people enter a dating relationship, they come together with their unique baggage: fallen shaping influences given to them by Adam, others, and their personal choices. After you commingle their baggage, there is no way to avoid sinful combustion in the home.

As you have probably surmised, you and your spouse are sinners. You not only came from your respective mothers' wombs speaking lies (Psalm 58:3), but you created a whole lot of baggage before you met each other. Some of your baggage was your doing, while other individuals heaped their troubles upon you. Either way, you both came together with more luggage than Samsonite. Perhaps you did not perceive all the issues during your dating relationship, and your premarriage counseling may have been inadequate, which it can be. Strangers marry each other. Too often, no one has the courage, grace, wisdom, or competence to speak into the lives of engaged couples. And to tell the truth, the newly minted couple is in love, so there is very little anyone could say to them anyway, right?

You left your baggage at the dating door and didn't pick it up again until you were six months into your marriage. If you have been a wise, humble, and teachable couple, you have sought help for your marriage. You know that the best sanctification happens in a community, so you gravitate toward companions who are willing and able to speak into your lives. Sometimes, couples do not seek help early enough, and after being married for more than a decade, they cannot keep their problems under wraps any longer. Their marriage problems begin to overpower their ability to keep things tamped down. Later, the couple's nest begins to empty as their children become older, and they are still without a sin plan—a pathway to repentance and transformation. The children are no longer a distraction, and the struggling couple has to decide between four options:

- Find help.
- Get a divorce.
- Create distractions like ministry, hobbies, or grandchildren.
- Coexist in a house that is not a home, waiting for the other to die.

My appeal to any couple in marriage trouble, regardless of the length of their marriage, is to find help. God's grace is greater than the problems, no matter how complex you think your problems are. The Bible has a lot to say about working through conflict. There is a plan for sin, and it begins with the gospel. The only requirement is humility, which creates teachability (James 4:6). Though you may have begun on the wrong foot, it does not mean you have to stay that way. God came to redeem and restore what we cannot fix. Redeeming broken things is at the heart of the gospel. If your marriage needs to change, I appeal to you to get help today!

## Time to Reflect

- Are you still surprised that your spouse sins? If so, why are you surprised when a fallen person falls?
- Rather than being frustrated by your spouse's imperfections, what is one way you can cooperate with God in helping your spouse mature into Christlikeness (Galatians 6:1-2)?

## Practical Suggestion

Write out a specific and practical plan based on your reflections regarding this devotion. If you and your spouse need help, will you contact a leader in your church to come alongside you both to restore the broken things in the marriage?

# 6

# Marriage Like This

Therefore a man shall leave his father and mother
and hold fast to his wife, and the two shall become
one flesh.

(Ephesians 5:31)

A husband and wife are not just two people within the
marriage. Yes, they have independent relationships with
the Lord and with others, but they are also one flesh. Like
our blessed Trinity, there is perfect oneness that unites the
Father, Son, and Spirit. This kind of union is both a mystery
and a practical reality. Though we cannot fully understand
what a one-flesh union means, we can functionally and
faithfully participate in a one-flesh marriage while enjoying
its benefits. Before two people made a one-flesh covenant
(agreement) with God, they were two individuals belonging
to different family units. At some point after their initial
introduction, they realized that being with each other
was worth leaving their respective families to set up their
unique autonomous domestic empire.

A family is not just when a couple has children but
when a couple is married. The first family unit was Adam
and Eve. They later added children to their autonomous
domestic empire. This newly formed family of two agreed
they would honor, cherish, love, and serve each other until
death separated their one flesh union. At the beginning

of any marital covenant, the couple is, for the most part, two different entities. Though on paper, they are one flesh under God and before the world, they are yet unable to fully enjoy all the benefits of being one flesh. With time, grace, community, and intentionality, it will be possible for them to mature into a God-husband-wife harmonic union, experiencing authentic koinonia. Not being able to entirely enjoy what it means to be one flesh is similar to our relationship with the Lord.

After your second birth ( John 3:7), you received everything needed to be Christlike (2 Peter 1:3; Ephesians 4:22-24). However, the functional working out of the fullness that God intends for you to enjoy takes a while to enjoy thoroughly (Philippians 2:12; 2 Peter 3:18). One flesh living is a lifelong journey. From your first introduction to your future separation at death, your lives should be an ever-unfolding mystery that incrementally reveals itself as you navigate the contours of life together. The idea of living in a one-flesh marriage is like many petals on a flower that open up and mature through time. It is an unfolding and assimilation of mind, body, soul, spirit, emotions, will, strengths, weaknesses, and more. Here are some of the goals a married couple moves toward as they begin to mature into a practical one-flesh union. Begin each descriptor with, "We are one in..."

| Desires | Words | Hobbies |
|---|---|---|
| Passions | Manners | Expectations |
| God Affection | Relationships | Fun |
| Parenting | Tastes | Intimacy |
| Finances | Interpretations | Prayer |

| Plans | Aspirations | Choices |
|---|---|---|
| Thoughts | Ideas | Dreams |
| Friendships | Forgiveness | Humor |
| Confession | [Husband Adds] | [Wife Adds] |

A man and a woman are different in many ways, particularly as it pertains to their personalities, strengths, weaknesses, and gifts. To be one flesh does not mean they are a carbon copy of each other. It means all of their positives and negatives, strengths and weaknesses blend into a unified, harmonic, God-centered, other-centered, one flesh union. What Adam was missing, Eve supplied. What Eve was missing, Adam provided. Like gears perfectly meshing into each other to make the machine function at an optimal level, the husband and wife mesh into each other so they can present a God-glorifying symmetry as a sweet savor to the Lord and blessing to each other and a testimony to others. Being different does not have to displace unity. Because of the grace of God, your differences within your one-flesh union should create richness and wholeness. Just like in the Trinity, there is a place for differences within the unity.

## Time to Reflect

Think about the one-flesh list above. Both spouses can add to it. Which ones stuck out to you? What other one-flesh traits would you add to the list?

## Practical Suggestion

Over the next few days, talk to your spouse about the traits that stood out to you. Talk about those in which you are truly maturing as a one-flesh couple. Discuss how you both can become one in some of the other traits. Will you make a practical plan and hold one another accountable for accomplishing the plan?

# 7

# No More Condemnation

*There is therefore now no condemnation for those who are in Christ Jesus.*

(Romans 8:1)

- How honest can you be with your spouse?
- Is your marriage vulnerable and safe enough to communicate transparently?
- Are you free from critique and condemnation, which releases you to be vulnerable?

A good way to consider my questions is to reflect upon how you relate to the Lord. I suspect you are honest, transparent, and vulnerable with Him. You freely talk to Him (prayer), and He freely talks to you (Bible). He knows you through and through, and though your relationship is not perfect, you are in a safe place as you mature with Him. Because of your call to imitate God, you have a remarkable opportunity to export your relationship with the Lord to your spouse (Ephesians 5:1; Philippians 4:9). Think for a moment about what it could look like if you chose to imitate God in your marriage. Let's focus on only one of the ways God relates to you: He does not condemn you. God never condemns, mocks, criticizes, or puts you down when you share your heart with Him (Ephesians 4:29). He is always ready to listen and willing to help. The Father knows your frame and understands your weaknesses. He encourages you by speaking into your various situations with love (Psalm 103:12-14).

- I'm sure you understand and appreciate this characteristic of the Lord, but how does it work out in your marriage?
- Have you ever put something out there for your spouse to hear, only to quickly retract it because unkindness and disinterest met your moment of transparency?
- Have you both created pockets of silence in your marriage because it's easier not to speak to each other than to enter into an arduous conversation?

Many couples are like this. They are more free on social media or with their friends than with their spouses. They have forgotten this core tenet of the gospel: Christ has removed our condemnation. If you have lost that gospel edge, it is time to reclaim your relational regression by asking God to redeem your marriage. You and your spouse are not static beings; you're always moving in one direction or the other. Either you are drifting apart, or you are intentionally pressing into each other. If you are drifting from each other, it will only grow worse. You will fill your pockets of silence with other things like children, work, hobbies, and even church. The key to restoring your marriage to gospel priorities begins by using your tongue for redemptive purposes rather than destructive ones (Ephesians 4:29). Christ came to transform lives, and we are supposed to be on His transformation team. Are you? The first place to begin restoring lives is with those closest to you. That person is your spouse.

## Time to Reflect

As you think through the condemnation aspects of your marriage, the questions below can apply to either of you.

1. When your spouse shares their heart with you, is your posture inviting and desirous to learn more?
2. Are you quick to give an answer, or are you quick to listen while asking clarifying questions so you can understand (James 1:19)?
3. How often do you ask your spouse about their secret thoughts? Do you seek to explore them with your spouse appropriately?
4. Do you see your spouse as an inexhaustible discovery to be enjoyed or as an exhausting human being?
5. Do your spouse's weaknesses get on your nerves? How are you discipling your spouse through those weaknesses?

## Practical Suggestion

Share the answers to these questions with your spouse. Be specific and practical when sharing any areas where you need to change with your spouse. You should write down your thoughts before you have this discussion. Ask the Father to give you the clarity you need to self-assess and communicate well with your spouse.

# 8

# For Your Spouse

What, then, shall we say to these things? If God is
for us, who can be against us?
(Romans 8:31)

Therefore be imitators of God, as beloved children.
And walk in love, as Christ loved us and gave himself
up for us, a fragrant offering and sacrifice to God.
(Ephesians 5:1-2)

If you are going to imitate the Lord in your marriage
(Ephesians 5:1), being for your spouse must be a logical
and loving objective and practice. That is how Paul talked to
the Romans about the Lord's attitude toward them. He said
God was for them. God is for you, too. Think for a moment
about how God is for you and how that motivates you to
love Him. God being for us is one of the most significant
highlights of the gospel. He is the one person we cannot
have against us. Before Paul told the Christians in Rome
that God was for them in Romans 8:31, the apostle provided
a few practical examples of how God was for them (Romans
8:29-30). He talked about God's active goodness on behalf of
those He loves. Here is how he said it:

For those whom he foreknew he also predestined to
be conformed to the image of his Son, in order that

he might be the firstborn among many brothers. And those whom he predestined he also called, and those whom he called he also justified, and those whom he justified he also glorified.

(Romans 8:29-30)

They were not left to wonder about God being for them. Based on His prior activity, they understood and felt the assurance of His love. He foreknew them, predestined them, called them, justified them, and glorified them. Do you remember the context in which Paul wrote the Book of Romans? People were killing the Christians in Rome. It was a public slaughter, a time of horrific, personal disappointment and defeat. The culture had turned against them, and Paul wanted the believers to know they were not alone: God was there. God was actively working in their lives. God was for them. Not only does Paul remind them of what the good Lord did (vs. 29-30) by bringing them to the point where they could clearly see God's activity in their lives (vs. 31), but he continued to hammer the gospel nail by repeatedly reminding them of Sovereign God's protective care. (Read Romans 8:32-39.)

Speaking about God's love for them only once was not enough for Paul. He believed in gospel redundancy—using different words and ways to say the same thing until his audience not only understood what he was saying but that knowledge transformed them. What better thing could you give to your spouse? If the Lord is for your undeserving spouse and you are for your undeserving spouse, your spouse is in the best place any human could be. The two greatest things that could ever happen to a couple is for them to live in the overflowing awareness of God's unmerited pleasure in them because of Christ while exporting and experiencing each other's undeniable affection for each other.

## Time to Reflect

You would do well to follow Paul's example by examining your heart regarding how you think about and treat your spouse. These questions will aid you as you consider the gospel and its practical outworking in your marriage.

1. Is your spouse assured of your love based on your actions (James 1:22)? Please explain.
2. How can you practice gospel redundancy when it comes to loving your spouse? I'm speaking of the repeated, practical reminders of your affection for them.

## Practical Suggestion

Ask the Spirit to illuminate your mind so you can see where you may need to adjust your attitude and actions toward your spouse. Ask the Father to give you the power to set aside what you want while enabling you to provide Christ practically to your spouse. Be prepared to write down the thoughts that come to mind. Take your soul to task while resisting all temptations to make this about what your spouse has done to you. You can address their need to change later. As you complete this project, invite your spouse into the process to discuss your thoughts with them, with plans to change.

# 9

# Who Pays for Sin?

*All we like sheep have gone astray; we have turned—*
*every one—to his own way; and the LORD has laid*
*on him the iniquity of us all.*

(Isaiah 53:6)

When your spouse sins, who pays for it? Do you make them pay for what they did wrong, or do you take your spouse to Jesus and show them how His death is enough punishment to remove all of our transgressions? Christians understand the point of the gospel: Christ paid for our sins. The profundity of the gospel encapsulated in five monosyllabic words is amazing grace! This simple way of explaining things is how we taught our children. I would hold up my right hand so they could see each finger. Starting at one end, I showed them the gospel. Five fingers. Five powerful words: Christ. Paid. For. My. Sins. When Adam chose to walk away from God by believing a lie (Genesis 3:6), God instituted a plan to redeem Adam and his fallen race (Genesis 3:15). Adam could not save himself. If God did not intervene, Adam and the rest of us would spend a Christless eternity in Hell.

No sin can go unpunished. Even nonbelievers understand the cause and effect of sins and the need for justice. Though they get it wrong much of the time and excuse their sins nearly all the time, they intuitively know the need to punish wrongs. Believers should praise God for the eternal freedom that comes from Christ's forever payment for sin, but there is something more profound than our present freedom and future hope.

- Are you living in the present freedom that Christ provides while resting in the future hope of guiltless glorification (1 Corinthians 1:8)?
- How are you exporting the guiltless, glorious gospel to your spouse?
- Do you lead your spouse to the payment maker after they sin against you?
- Do you make your spouse pay for their sins, or do you help them get to the restorative Jesus?

Christ does not make you pay for your sins if you are a Christian. He sacrificed Himself for your sin by giving His life for you. He does not get angry at you but seeks to restore you (Galatians 6:1-2). If you truly understand this fundamental gospel truth at the moment of your spouse's sin, your response should be a gospel-motivated sacrifice rather than a self-centered punishment. Rather than choosing sinful anger (punishment) as a response to your spouse's sin, you must adopt an attitude of forgiveness (sacrifice). Jumping to sinful anger will distort and strain your relationship with God and with your spouse.

If your goal is for your spouse to walk in holiness, you have to think and act like Christ (1 Corinthians 11:1). To help your spouse to be like Christ, you will have to set aside what you want at this moment. If you choose to punish your spouse when they sin, do not expect to have a one-flesh union that glorifies God or benefits either of you. Each time you punish your spouse, you are making it harder to accomplish the thing you desire the most for your marriage: to be Christlike. If the gospel means anything to you, it must be real at the moment of sin, whether yours or your spouse's. Otherwise, you are mocking the redemptive purpose of His sacrifice.

## Time to Reflect

1.  How does the redemptive power of the gospel impact your marriage at the moment of your spouse's sin? Are there any growth opportunities or things you want to change about yourself?
2.  When your spouse sins against you, do you punish or sacrifice? Please explain.

## Practical Suggestion

Share this devotional with your spouse. Tell them how the Spirit of God illuminated your thinking, specifically by how you treat your spouse's sin. Pray together, asking the Father to help you help your spouse. Talk about a practical way to implement this devotion into your marriage.

# 10

# Something Between Us

*And Jesus cried out again with a loud voice and yielded up his spirit.*

(Matthew 27:50)

I was meeting with a couple who seemed convinced that the other person in the marriage was the biggest sinner in the room. Both of them were clear about how the other spouse was sabotaging their relationship. They had their facts straight, and, for the most part, they were correct in their accusations. It did not matter what angle I took to motivate them to think and act like Christians. Finally, after several attempts to convince them of the futility of their positions, I conceded any further hope of a ceasefire. There would be no redemptive-relational progress that day. They were too mad, too self-justified, too hurt, too unforgiving, and too stubborn to change. At that point, I gave up and recommended that the combatants continue their conflict. Yes, I told them to pursue their anger toward each other. "Keep on keeping on. Duke it out." I paused and added, "But under one condition, I want to make a stipulation." I said they could continue to fight all they wanted to as long as I could choose the location for all future skirmishes.

I continued: "I want you to climb Golgotha's bloody hill, where the multitudes scorned our dying Savior, and His Father judged Him on Adam's tree (Matthew 27:32-44). I want you to go to Calvary, the place where the crucified Son of God became sin for you and me—the place where the Sovereign Judge punished all our sins (2 Corinthians 5:21)." Christ took this Christian couple's sin by willingly giving up His life to the scorching judgment of His Father. Jesus' actions gave this sparring pair a free pass, so to speak; God would never eternally judge them for their past, present, and future sins (John 8:36; Romans 8:1). I further appealed to them as they prepared to duke it out to position their bodies in such a way that the cross of Christ would be in their sightlines. My hope was for them to get so close to the cross that the blood of the dying Lamb could figuratively drop on them as they sought to bite and devour each other (Galatians 5:15).

Then I added that it would benefit them to intentionally, on occasion, glance at that cross during their conflict so that while they were wounding each other, they would be able to be reminded of the One who was wounded for their transgressions (Isaiah 53:5). I hoped that the wooden beam (Matthew 7:3-5) would become an impediment to their blows, that they would have to figuratively stretch around the cross to inflict further pain on their spouse. I wanted the cross to always be in their sightlines, especially as their anger toward each other escalated. As things stood, the cross was not preeminent in their thinking. Christ, at best, was on the periphery of their lives as they persisted in their argumentation and criticalness. I wanted them to visually discern and viscerally experience the historical fact of the dying Lamb of God. I hoped God's Spirit would burn the gospel deep into their minds and prick their hearts. I wanted them to be affected by the horrible realities of the cross of Christ.

## Time to Reflect

1. How does the cross of Christ influence your arguments with your spouse? Please explain.
2. How easy (or difficult) is it for you to know the truths of the cross while holding on to unforgiveness toward your spouse?
3. How does the cross steer you from judgment and condemning thoughts toward your spouse?

## Practical Suggestion

What is your favorite song about the cross? If you don't have one, I recommend "When I Survey the Wondrous Cross," which is a classic. I want you to memorize a gospel-rich cross song and sing it to yourself throughout your day while asking the Lord to affect you by the death of Christ. Let His death grip and transform your soul. May the cross come between the two of you. Will you and your spouse sing a cross song aloud together?

# 11

# Strengths and Weaknesses

*Do nothing from rivalry or conceit, but in humility count others more significant than yourselves.*
*(Philippians 2:3)*

One of the most powerful ways to imitate Jesus in our marriages is by having an other-worldly lack of self-interest (Philippians 2:5-11). A profound statement that connects so well with the gospel is that if the gospel truly anchors us, we have nothing to fear, nothing to defend, nothing to lose, and nothing to hide. Isn't Jesus like that with you? He is so secure in His relationship with you that any angry frustration from you or the other ways in which you express your disappointments to Him do not manage Him. He is not a manipulatable person, no matter how anyone responds to Him. We have said all sorts of sordid things to Him, but His soul is as sturdy as ever. The reason is simple: Jesus is about redemption and restoration of fallen souls rather than Himself. He dramatically proved this by going to the cross in our place. Though we should never be angry with God, and I'm definitely not recommending it, it is possible, and if that were the case, our anger would never disorient Him or sever the relationship we have with Him.

He eagerly listens to us and loves us in response (Romans 5:8; 1 John 4:8). That kind of love is what husbands and wives should model for each other.

**INSECURITY ILLUSTRATED:** Biff is immature and insecure. If Mable says anything that relates to him, their marriage, and the need for him to change, Biff takes it personally and usually sulks for days in response to her remarks. Mable does not believe she can be completely honest with him because of his insecurities. Biff's reactive demeanor causes her to take a guarded posture. Rather than speaking openly and honestly about what is going on between them, it is more like talking to a child, where Mable must weigh and measure every word before she shares it (John 16:2). Mable is pulling double duty: she must care for her soul and care for her husband's, too. She has to grow him up before he can contribute to her sanctification or their marriage.

Mable works hard not to be self-righteous about Biff, but it is a challenge. Biff is a weak, immature, and insecure husband. He does not process things through a biblical lens, as his shaping influences have captured him. He responds to things through his past personal experiences and hurts. His dad was a mean and condemning man who had a significant influence on Biff's life. Biff is a tedious man who weighs heavily on Mable's soul. She grows weary when around him because of his longstanding insecurity. There is ongoing and seemingly unresolvable in-equitableness in their relationship. It is similar to a college student married to an eighth grader. Biff is so different from Christ and not getting any closer to Him. He esteems himself more than his wife, which sabotages his walk with God and his relationship with Mable.

## Time to Reflect

All Christians carry baggage from their former manner of life into their new creation that God is transforming them into. In most marriages, there is an in-equitableness in how the two partners are maturing in Christ, which makes sense because each Christian is unique, never in the same place as any other Christian, even if they are married to each other. It would be a monumental mistake to expect one spouse to be equal to the other.

1. In what ways are you different from your spouse?
2. Did you answer the question by highlighting your strengths and your spouse's weaknesses first, or did you think about your spouse's strengths and your weaknesses first?
3. If you thought about your strengths first, you might not have an other-worldly lack of self-interest like Christ. The danger is that if you think more about where you get it right and where your spouse gets it wrong, you might become angry, bitter, and unforgiving and resign to hopelessness, along with your pre-existing self-righteousness.

## Practical Suggestion

Share with your spouse one of your weaknesses and how you need their help working through it. Invite them to share similarly.

# 12

# The Most Effective Things

*Put off your old self, which belongs to your former manner of life and is corrupt through deceitful desires, and be renewed in the spirit of your minds, and put on the new self, created after the likeness of God in true righteousness and holiness.*

*(Ephesians 4:22-24)*

The modeling of Christ and practicing repentance in your home are at the top of the list of what you both should be doing in your family relationships. Suppose you are not imitating Christ or repenting of sins. In that case, your marriage can only limp along with a Band-Aid approach while accelerating the accumulative frustration that leftover, hungover sinning does until death disrupts your one-flesh union. There is no way to circumvent the hard and humble way of going to your spouse, confessing your sin, asking for forgiveness, and encouraging your spouse to have a similar kind of humility that forgiveness-granting exemplifies to the offender and offended. You will know if you have authentically buried the hatchet if you can talk about what happened in non-punitive ways. There is no biblical reason for a Christian couple not to repent and reconcile.

However, I suspect the overwhelming majority of those who name the name of Christ do not live out authentic, practical repentance in their marriages. Imagine this: After you have declared that you nailed your sin to Jesus' cross, you can start doing the grace-empowered work of examining what went wrong, why it went wrong, and how to avoid repeating the offense. Where else in God's world can the offended collaborate in the sanctification of the offender for the ongoing restorative development of their marriage? Real-life change is a stunning turn of events for fallen people. It's one of the best-kept secrets in Christian families and the local churches they attend. If you are a practitioner of full repentance, keep on doing what you have been doing. Repentance is a gift from the Lord (2 Timothy 2:24-25). Don't ever let up. Refine it. Ensure it is reflexive repentance: as soon as you sin, you name it and claim it, and your spouse does similarly by granting forgiveness and then moving on to the restoration of the relationship.

## Time to Reflect

Here are the 13 steps to authentic, biblical repentance in sequential order. I've labeled and defined each step for you. As you read through the list, will you answer the questions provided?

1. **SIN:** What does it mean to have clearly defined sin categories rather than ambiguous labels for the things you do wrong?
2. **GUILT:** Do you understand that all sin brings guilt, whether you know it or not? Once you transgress God's Word, you are automatically guilty before God.
3. **CONVICTION:** Do you have a biblically informed conscience that experiences the Spirit's sweet conviction? We should feel our transgressions.

4. **CONFESSION:** After you sin, do you agree with God (and anyone else you sinned against) that you transgressed?

5. **PRE-FORGIVENESS:** When your spouse sins against you, do you quickly become ready to forgive your spouse?

6. **FORGIVENESS:** When you sin, do you seek to transact forgiveness with your spouse? It is a transactional request for forgiveness.

7. **POST-FORGIVENESS:** Does the power of the gospel neutralize the offense between both of you so you can reconcile?

8. **RECONCILE:** After you ask for and receive forgiveness, are you able to talk about what happened?

9. **RESTORATION:** With the sin behind you, do you actively seek to keep from doing it again? Please explain how you have done this in the past.

10. **PUT OFF:** Do your sin categories give you the insight and clarity you need to know what to put off?

11. **RENEW YOUR MIND:** As you put off the offense, are you training your inner person not to do it again? How does this happen in your life and marriage?

12. **PUT ON:** What does it mean to put on Christ, practically speaking?

13. **DISCIPLE:** Active repentance is not just about getting better but about getting better so you can help others. Are you practically discipling others, including your spouse?

## Practical Suggestion

Answer the questions provided in the reflection section and assess your strengths and weaknesses. In the areas where you are weak, write out a specific plan to mature in those areas.

# 13

# Change One Thing

*So whoever knows the right thing to do and fails to do it, for him it is sin.*

(James 4:17)

What were the practical things you did when you first won your spouse's affections? Are you still doing them, or has the pace of life diverted your attention from your early marriage priorities? Reflect upon the giddy time in your relationship. Do you remember those carefree and silly days when it was just you two? Those days do not have to remain in your past. It was important to Lucia and me that we fight to keep the dating experience in our marriage experience. Because of God's grace, we still enjoy giddy, silly, carefree, and fun times in our relationship; we are still buddies, always working not to let anything come between us, including our children, our work, our church, or our sin. But it was not always this way. We did lose focus in our marriage. The moorings of a stable marriage broke loose, and we drifted from the God-centered practicalities of our covenant. We needed a severe marital realignment.

Thankfully, God imposed Himself into our marriage. He did for us what we could not do for ourselves: He changed us (2 Timothy 2:24-25). It did not happen overnight; it was two challenging years, but we fell in love with each other all over again. Though the pace of our lives is at an all-time high due to our ministry and the age of our children, those things do not disrupt our marriage priorities. With God's assistance, we fight to maintain today what we began while dating. Our goal is to behave like newlyweds until the Lord calls on death to separate us. That means we must continue to grab, touch, hold, hug, feel, and kiss each other like we did in the early days. But with a twist. In the beginning, we were young, somewhat silly, naive, and enjoyed intimacy because that is what young people do.

Today, our love is breathtakingly more mature. It's maturity between two individuals who have seen the devastating effect of selfishness and who have asked for and received God's forgiveness and restoration. If your marriage is declining, do not think another person will solve your problems. All another person will do is give you another ten or fifteen years to get back to the same place you are today. Hobbies or addictions are not the answer, either. Those things will lead you down a path of dissatisfaction to where nobody or nothing will be able to make you happy. Fortunately, the problem is closer to you and more within your control: it is in your heart.

Suppose you humbly confess whatever sins separate you from God and your spouse. In that case, the Lord will jump to your side to help restore your marriage (James 4:6). If sin keeps you from a romantically spiritual marriage, God has a solution and a desire to give you an incredible marriage restoration. I realize some spouses can be too hurt, too unforgiving, too stubborn, or too mean to make these changes. Spousal unwillingness does happen, and it makes things immeasurably hard for the willing spouse. My appeal is for you not to shortchange the grace of God by not trying to follow Him through the dark waters of an imperfect marriage. If not trusting Him by doing your thing has led to an unsatisfactory marriage, the best response you have is to make up your mind to follow Him now regardless of the cost, time involved, or disinterest of your spouse (Luke 14:28-33).

## Time to Reflect

What is one thing you will do to change yourself, with the hope the Lord will use your obedient faith to improve your marriage?

## Practical Suggestion

1. Ask God what that one thing is.
2. Write down what you believe He is leading you to change.
3. Make a realistic plan to change that thing about you.

# 14

# Conflict Resolution Tip

*First take the log out of your own eye, and then you will see clearly to take the speck out of your brother's eye.*

(Matthew 7:5)

A few years ago, I was counseling a couple who were angry with each other. During our counseling, I asked the wife what was wrong with the marriage. Without hesitation or skipping a beat, she gave me a long, clear, and detailed list of all the things that were wrong with her husband. There was no question about it: he was a failure. Because I like to play fair, I turned to the lady's husband and asked him about the state of their marriage. Without flinching or taking a breath, the husband gave me a list of all the things his wife had done wrong in their marriage. There was no question about it: she was a failure. Two people looking at the same thing had two completely different perspectives on how their marriage became such a dysfunctional mess.

Not to be discouraged because of their impeccable memories about what was wrong with their marriage, I turned back to the wife and asked her to give me a list of all the good things she appreciated about her husband. I asked the husband for a similar list regarding his wife. At that point, the most fascinating thing happened. Without warning and within seconds, both spouses were overcome with a severe case of amnesia. They could not think of anything. Because my combatants found themselves stuck in their self-imposed self-righteousness, I decided to take another angle to break the silence. I read Matthew 7:3-5 to them. I asked each spouse to list all the ways they had personally failed in their marriage. The one stipulation was that they could not add the word but to any of their reasons for their failures in the marriage.

Their log list was to include all overt and less discernible offenses that they had inflicted on each other. As they were building their log lists, I asked them to create a grace list. They were to write down all the good things they appreciated about their spouse and all the good things their spouse did in their marriage. I want to say that they did what I asked them to do, but that was not the case. It is rare for any couple to take this challenge if stubbornness, unforgiveness, and other pride-related strongholds have laid claim to their hearts. The gospel is radical by itself, but it is even more radical when two people begin to practicalize it in their lives. What about you? Has the gospel transformed you? There are two ways to assess yourself:

- Are you more aware of and more willing to identify your sin than the sin of your spouse?
- Are you more willing to be an encouragement to your spouse rather than a critic?

*If you love those who love you, what benefit is that to you? For even sinners love those who love them. And if you do good to those who do good to you, what benefit is that to you? For even sinners do the same. But love your enemies, and do good...for he is kind to the ungrateful and the evil.*

*(Luke 6:32-33, 35)*

## Time to Reflect

If you want to transform your marriage, here are four things you can do today:

1. Start a log list that is about you.
2. Start a grace list that is about your spouse.
3. Meet with your spouse to confess your log list while asking for forgiveness.
4. Share your grace list while thanking God for His work in the life of your spouse.

## Practical Suggestion

Start identifying and communicating all the evidences of grace that you see in your spouse (Ephesians 4:29). As the Lord reminds you of His gracious work in the life of your spouse, share those details to build up your spouse.

# 15

# Push Your Spouse to Christ

*But God shows his love for us in that while we were still sinners, Christ died for us.*

(Romans 5:8)

How do you positively or negatively contribute to your marriage? In broad categories, you can help in one of two ways, though you may contribute in both, depending on what is going on during any particular season of your marriage:

- You can motivate your spouse by grace.
- You can demotivate your spouse by sinful attitudes, words, or behaviors.

There are times that a spouse can be so hurt and so angry with their spouse—because of the ongoing disappointments from their spouse—that they do not see their sinful contributions to the marriage. Those are the sad situations where the person shuts out the Spirit of God from the marriage (Ephesians 4:30; 1 Thessalonians 5:19). The mounting disappointment is overwhelming, and the spouses are more about grenade launching than redemptive communication (Ephesians 4:29).

- For the wife, it will almost always be in the area of respect. Nothing will cut the heart out of a husband like a wife's disrespectful attitude or tongue. Her husband is wired to lead, but because of sin, his temptation is to lead poorly, especially in their marriage. I am sorry it is this way, but too often, that is the case. He needs his wife's assistance for him to lead well.
- For the husband, it is mostly about love and protection. Nothing will cut the heart out of a wife like a husband who is lazy in his love and his protective care. If he does not love his wife well, he is contributing to her steady distancing from the marriage (Ephesians 5:28-29). Though she is responsible for her choice to distance herself, he is responsible for his sinful contribution to her actions.

The answer for the husband and the wife is to think about each other the way Christ thinks about them. Christ loves imperfect people, and He is always busy working on their behalf, seeking to redeem and transform them into His likeness. Is your spouse imperfect? Does that surprise you? It should not. Scripture's testimony is far less flattering regarding the human condition. Your spouse deserves to go to Hell. Nothing speaks to their worthlessness like the outcome for all spouses who have not been born a second time (John 3:7; Romans 3:12; Revelation 20:15). The good news is how the gospel penetrates our nonsense and gives us something undeserved. The gospel gives spouses empowering favor, too (James 3:6). What they get is not based upon their behaviors (Isaiah 64:6) but upon the grace, mercy, and love of God (Ephesians 2:8-9; Titus 3:5). You are to live with your spouse by imitating Christ's redemptive behavior to your spouse (1 Corinthians 11:1). Christ does not put things in your way to demotivate you to live for His glory. He is not annoying or aggravating. He draws you by

His love. He overcomes your nonsense by keeping His eye on a better prize (Hebrews 12:2; Philippians 3:14). Christ is a transformer whose purpose is to transform your life. Even being despised and rejected by others did not deter Him from His restorative goals for your life (Isaiah 53:3; Galatians 6:1-2).

## Time to Reflect

1. Think about how what you should be doing for your spouse is what Christ does for you.
2. How has your behavior positively or adversely contributed to the state of your marriage?
3. Does your spouse feel encouraged to be around you? Will you ask your spouse? What was their response?

## Practical Suggestion

These are excellent examination questions that will identify what may be going on in your heart while revealing how you contribute to your marriage. Though your spouse is entirely responsible for their actions, God calls you to love your spouse in such a way that contributes to their sanctification. How is the Spirit asking you to respond to this devotion?

# 16

# Setting Aside Your Desires

*Do nothing from rivalry or conceit, but in humility count others more significant than yourselves. Let each of you look not only to his own interests, but also to the interests of others.*
*(Philippians 2:3-4)*

The most significant problem hindering humble discipleship in a marriage is self-centeredness. Too many spouses demand and manipulate what they want while relegating their role of discipling their spouse to a tertiary consideration. Nothing will blow up a marriage quicker than a lack of other-centeredness, a mindset that is contrary to the gospel. Jesus set aside His desires to help broken people. Discipleship is every spouse's responsibility. Christ took on the form of a servant to transform damaged individuals (Philippians 2:5-10). A large part of my marriage counseling is spent pressing this kind of gospel thinking into the minds of the couple in trouble. Not until they understand and apply the other-centered force of the gospel will they have a genuinely satisfying biblical marriage. You can't fix your marriage by yelling louder or demanding more. Adamic fallenness has completely and utterly broken down your spouse, and they need your help to overcome those fallen shaping influences. In this way, your marriage is more about your spouse and Adam than you. Your spouse has a preexisting Adamic condition. To live out this gospel-informed worldview, here are six helpful ideas to give you an idea of what it looks like in your marriage.

1. **CONCUR:** Agree that your spouse is part of Adam's fallen race and not entirely sanctified. There are things wrong that need your discipleship care. Do you know how to address those things humbly?
2. **CONFESS:** Do you know how to lead your spouse by removing your complicating problems from the marriage? Make sure you are not compounding your spouse's problems by adding yours to the pile.
3. **COMMUNICATE:** Now that you are no longer part of the problem, start talking to your spouse about how to best serve them in their sanctification. What is your redemptive plan for your spouse's sanctification?
4. **COLLABORATE:** Your collaboration must be practical and reciprocal. Be specific about how you want to serve your spouse. How are you motivating your spouse to be like you as you follow Christ (1 Corinthians 11:1)?
5. **COMMUNITY:** Let others into your marriage. You both need a grace-filled community to help bring long-term, sustaining change. Bring your marriage into the light of a small community of friends. Who are the friends who are helping your marriage?
6. **CONTINUE:** You must turn these ideas into habits so you can express mutual repentance in your marriage. Let these things be a lifelong process.

As you continue to work together, here are twenty practical tips for your consideration.

1.   Confess your sin against your spouse soon after the sin.
2.   Rendezvous regularly to chat, whether on dates, at bedtime, or other contexts.
3.   Appropriately talk about your secret thoughts.
4.   Inquire about your spouse's thoughts.
5.   Have a consistent sex life.
6.   Pray for each other at different times during the day.
7.   Follow up on Sunday's sermon by asking application questions.
8.   Show affection in different venues, even in front of others.
9.   Grab, touch, and flirt with each other regularly.
10.  Kiss often.
11.  Discern evidence of God's work in your spouse's life and talk about it.
12.  Begin your sleep by being close to each other.
13.  Honor each other in public.
14.  Never talk critically about your spouse unless your spouse is there or aware and in agreement with you sharing with others.
15.  Share with your spouse what God is doing in your life regularly.
16.  Have lots of fun with each other.
17.  Laugh together.
18.  Hold hands.
19.  Ask your spouse their perspective on how you can mature.
20.  Let your spouse know when they observe your sin that you want them to provide corrective care.

## Time to Reflect

What is the hardest item on the list for you to do with your spouse? Why is it hard?

## Practical Suggestion

Make it your aim to change those things. This process begins by talking to God and, eventually, your spouse so you both can work on improving any snags in your marriage.

# 17

# Be an Excellent Spouse

Have this mind among yourselves, which is yours in Christ Jesus, who, though he was in the form of God, did not count equality with God a thing to be grasped, but emptied himself, by taking the form of a servant, being born in the likeness of men. And being found in human form, he humbled himself by becoming obedient to the point of death, even death on a cross. Therefore God has highly exalted him and bestowed on him the name that is above every name, so that at the name of Jesus every knee should bow, in heaven and on earth and under the earth, and every tongue confess that Jesus Christ is Lord, to the glory of God the Father.

(Philippians 2:5-11)

This devotion is in a three-part sequential order. The second step builds on the first, and the third relies upon the second. If you want to enjoy your marriage to the fullest, you must live out all three phases in the order presented.

# Will I Die?

There was a need on our planet. Humanity rebelled against God and became depraved without any hope of a course correction. Jesus, the only right solution, decided to give up what He had with His Father to rescue us. What Christ did is the gospel, which is the prototype for how humans are to relate to each other. In marriage, both spouses are obligated to set aside their desires for each other's mutual and reciprocal benefit. They imitate the gospel by cooperating with the Lord for His fame and their sanctification. There is always a sacrifice involved with ongoing care, and one of the most important questions you can ask is, "Will I die daily for my spouse?"

## Will I Sanctify?

Your spouse is damaged goods. The fall brought depravity into all our lives. You picked a partner from the dinged and dented section of the store. Of course, the whole store was full of dinged and dented individuals. There are no perfect people from whom to choose a spouse. To put it plainly, the person you married has issues. The call to marriage is a call to work, as both spouses put in a sweat of the brow work ethic to make the marriage look like Christ and His Church. Are you cooperating with the Lord in the sanctification of your damaged spouse?

## Will I Enjoy?

It is not a wrong motivation to work for the benefit of your labor. Some have said that love is an act without an expectation of anything in return. The Bible teaches a different perspective; there is a reward for work, which you should expect from your marriage. Jesus will receive the work of His hands (Hebrews 12:2; Ephesians 5:27). It does not have to be wrong to want to enjoy the benefits of your words and actions. However, it would be a mistake to demand benefits without doing the hard work to earn those benefits, and it would be wrong to sin against your spouse because they have yet to meet your expectations. The idea of sowing and reaping is not always negative. Are you enjoying the benefits of the work you have put into your marriage?

## Time to Reflect

1. **WILL YOU DIE?** Jesus set aside His life to create a better life for you. What does it look like to set aside what you want for the benefit of your spouse?
2. **WILL YOU SANCTIFY?** Jesus humbled Himself to the cross, which opened the door for your salvation and sanctification. How is the Lord using your humble obedience to sanctify your spouse?
3. **WILL YOU ENJOY?** Jesus' exaltation came after He set aside what He had and obediently gave His life for you. How have you benefited from the work you have put into your marriage?

## Practical Suggestion

Spend the next few days reflecting on Philippians 2:5-11 while asking the Lord to help you mature in any area where the gospel is weak in your life.

# 18

# Your Difficult Spouse

*Repay no one evil for evil, but give thought to do what is honorable in the sight of all. If possible, so far as it depends on you, live peaceably with all.*
(Romans 12:17-18).

There is a good chance your spouse is not everything you hoped for in a marriage. Of course, neither are you. Imperfect people have a way of disappointing imperfect people. Perchance your spouse is difficult at times to live with, here are seven things for you to practically apply to yourself and your marriage.

1.  **GOD LOVES YOU:** Loneliness in a difficult marriage keeps you alone. If you are not careful, you can begin to think the good Lord has left you, too. It is not true. God loves you, and your circumstances do not alter His love for you. Conditions can change you, but one of the Lord's many attributes is His immutability: He never changes (Malachi 3:6; Hebrews 13:8).

2.  **YOUR SPOUSE IS CAUGHT:** Paul would say something has caught your spouse (Galatians 6:1). Imagine

if you were walking through the woods and found your spouse ensnared around the ankle by a bear trap. Your spouse is caught in sin and cannot extricate themself from it. Their caught-ness does not excuse the behavior or prohibit you from confronting it, but it does help you to understand there's a greater issue in play (Galatians 6:1-2).

3.  **YOU ARE TO RESTORE:** Paul wants you to give serious thought to how you respond to your spouse. If you walked up on your spouse caught in a bear trap in the forest, how would you respond? Would you become angry because something caught your spouse, or would you try to gently restore them while keeping watch on your soul so you do not become tempted to sin?

4.  **FIND SOME HELP:** Because of your spouse's habituation to a pattern of challenges and your vulnerability to sin against them, you must reach out for help. Do not go through this alone. Regardless of your spouse's desire to control you, find someone to walk with you through this process. Even the Bible's call to submission does not prevent you from helping a caught person.

5.  **PREPARE FOR THE LONG HAUL:** I do not know if your spouse will ever change. I do know there are several situations in the Bible where the Lord allowed sin to continue in peoples' lives. Paul's thorn in the flesh (2 Corinthians 12:7-10), the story of Joseph (Genesis 50:20), as well as the story of Pharaoh (Exodus 9:16; Romans 9:17) are three examples. The most profound illustration of God allowing sin for His greater purposes is when He crushed His Son on the cross (Isaiah 53:10).

6.  **PRAY WITHOUT CEASING:** Though I am not sure your spouse will change, there is no question the Lord is

calling you to an other-world reliance on Him (2 Corinthians 1:8-9). You cannot fix your spouse (1 Corinthians 3:6). I know you know this, but I want to state it clearly, and you need to remind yourself of this truth over and over again. Your most compelling call to action is to pray (1 Thessalonians 5:17).

7. **GUARD YOUR HEART:** Guard your heart with all diligence because what flows out of it will determine the course of your life (Proverbs 4:23; Luke 6:45). Your marriage will be a temptation for you to sin because of the ongoing disappointment. How self-aware are you of your thoughts? Do you hear how you speak to others about your marriage? Do your close friends agree that you're guarding your heart?

## Time to Reflect

Your gratitude will affect your attitude. It is a quirky saying, but you will remember it, and if you apply the tagline to your life, it will begin to change you regardless of what happens to your spouse.

## Practical Suggestion

If you are predisposed to journaling, write out your grateful thoughts each day and present them to the Lord. Paul had a habit of being grateful to mean-spirited individuals (1 Corinthians 1:4). Rehearse your list of things that make you grateful daily. Ensure your spouse is on your gratitude list, and as the Lord brings more things to be grateful for your spouse, add them to your list.

# 19

# The Reciprocal Marriage

*If one member suffers, all suffer together; if one member is honored, all rejoice together.*

*(1 Corinthians 12:26)*

Biff and Mable married 13 years ago. Most of those years were difficult. Mable struggles with insecurity, which has played out in their marriage by her keeping tabs on Biff. He calls her a nag. Her deeper insecurity is born out of something that Biff did not cause, which is why he sees her interrogations and accusations as a burden. Rather than discerning Mable as an opportunity to shepherd her, he responds by drifting farther from her, which puts their marriage in an unresolvable, circular trap.

1. The more he drifts from her, the more concerned she becomes.
2. The more concerned she becomes, the more she nags.
3. The more she nags, the more he drifts from her.

Eventually, Biff committed adultery, and Mable's fears came to pass. The thing she dreaded—losing Biff—

happened. It was a self-fulfilling prophecy. How did they arrive at this place in their marriage? How could they have built their marriage on a better foundation?

## What Men Want

To answer these questions, you have to go back to God's original design for the male and female and how the effects of sin altered His intent. The Lord made Adam for Himself (Genesis 2:7). He created Adam in His image (leader) and gave him things to do (work). From Adam's perspective, it was a perfect world. He basked in the glory of the Lord and spent his time doing things for the Lord. God intrinsically tied Adam's identity to two things: leading and doing. Adam led his world and did things in his world. Whenever you degrade a man's leadership and ability to perform, you destroy the man. Men know it is emasculating not to be able to work and provide for others. Adam was a leading man who worked for the Lord while living in God's satisfying pleasure. Then God surveyed the scene of Adam's life and decided he needed to do more than lead by working in the garden. Adam needed someone to complement him—a companion and counterpart. Thus, the Lord made Eve (Genesis 2:18).

## What Women Want

Eve was not like Adam. She came from his side, not from the dirt (Genesis 2:7). She looked different and was expected to serve a different role. The Lord did not make Eve for Himself but for Adam (Genesis 2:22-25). When a man receives a gift from the Lord, he is expected to care for it (Ephesians 5:29). It was no longer proper for Adam to think that working in the garden, away from home, was all that mattered. Eve was part of his ever-increasing responsibilities. Adam had to lead and provide for Eve (1 Peter 3:7). There is a vulnerability to a woman that is strikingly different from a man. God made her this way because of what she is called to do: follow, submit, and serve her husband. This begs a paramount question: if you had to follow, submit, and serve someone, what are the necessary assurances you need from the one leading you?

- Will you love me?
- Will you protect me?

Put yourself in Eve's fig-bottom shoes. If you had to hook your wagon to a man, what would you be thinking? "If I have to submit to your leadership and provision, you better love and protect me."

## Time to Reflect

Spouses live on a continuum, where the husband leads, and the wife follows. Their lives are also circular, where each person is dependent upon the other. The reciprocality and mutual dependence of the two give strength to their one-flesh union.

## Practical Suggestion

1.  Husband, what is one way you need to change your leadership and provision for your spouse that will give her assurance of your love and protective care?
2.  Wife, what is one way you can use your words to motivate your husband to be a more effective leader and provider, especially if he is not doing well at this time?

# 20

# Help Your Spouse Change

*Do you presume on the riches of his kindness and forbearance and patience, not knowing that God's kindness is meant to lead you to repentance?*
(Romans 2:4)

There are several ways to motivate your spouse to change. Here are six awful examples. As you go through this list, examine your heart to see which ones you tend to employ the most often when your spouse is not changing and maturing according to your expectations.

- **THE SHAME APPROACH:** Pointing out how dumb that thing was that your spouse did.
- **THE GUILT APPROACH:** Comparing your spouse's poor behavior with someone else's good behavior.
- **THE THREAT APPROACH:** Yelling the consequences of your spouse's sin if they continue in it.
- **THE CONDEMNATION APPROACH:** Putting your spouse down or making fun of them in front of others.
- **THE CRITICAL APPROACH:** Always pointing out your spouse's faults, no matter how small they may be.
- **THE CYNICAL APPROACH:** Though your spouse may

have done something good, you know their intent was selfish.

How did you do? Did you see yourself using any of those approaches? All of the methods I have suggested can work, especially if your spouse willingly gives you that kind of power over them or if you manipulate them into submission. If any of these methods are the ones you employ, you may be a domineering and exasperating person. If you continue to use these methods, your marriage will stay weak, strained, and non-redemptive. Let's say your observations about your spouse are correct. Having the right perspective does not automatically mean your methods for change are correct. The Bible contains a process for change that can be redemptively useful. This approach finds its anchor in the gospel, and though there are many ways to say it, I am going to simplify by calling it "being an encourager." How are you doing at encouraging your spouse, especially when they are not meeting your expectations? (cf. Matthew 5:44-45; Luke 6:27).

Your primary motive for being an encourager should be your desire to magnify God's name by displaying His Son in the context of your marriage. You want to make His name fantastically great for His glory and the benefit of your spouse. If you obtain good results because you were kind to your spouse, you can praise God for the pleasing results. Personal blessings that happen for loving God and others as you love yourself are a thing to be praised, not an idol to be worshiped. Potential impure motivations are why you want to guard your heart against using encouragement as a tool rather than being obedient regardless of outcomes. The Encouragement Approach does not mean you should overlook sin. You should not ignore your spouse's sins, though finding fault is not typically that hard. You may have to train your mind by breaking strongholds to encourage your spouse. Adamic people do not natively make encouragement their practice. But when you do encourage, redemptive things happen.

- Your spouse is encouraged.
- Your spouse gains insight into how Jesus lived.
- Your spouse learns good and acceptable behaviors.
- You both can praise God for His work in your lives.
- The encouraged spouse is built up in the faith.
- You strengthen your relationship with your spouse.
- You have more liberty to bring future critique to your spouse.

## Time to Reflect

Do you have a well-tuned Got-It-Right antenna? As you might imagine, this habit takes more time and is harder to perfect than being a nitpicker. Catching people doing well takes effort, but when you do catch them getting it right, it motivates them toward change because that is what God's kindness does.

## Practical Suggestion

For the next seven days, I want you to sharpen your Got-It-Right antenna by observing, catching, identifying, and acknowledging your spouse getting it right. Each time you catch your spouse doing something good, let them know. Work hard at becoming an encourager.

# 21

# Your Crisis Communication

*Count it all joy, my brothers, when you meet trials of various kinds, for you know that the testing of your faith produces steadfastness. And let steadfastness have its full effect, that you may be perfect and complete, lacking in nothing.*

(James 1:2-4).

There are at least two parts to every crisis: what is happening to you in real time and space and what is spiritually happening inside of you as the Lord matures you through the trial. The first part is usually discernible to anyone associated with the crisis. The second part is not as perceptible to the person in the crisis or those observing the crisis. Typically, when I am experiencing a crisis, I can articulate what I am going through and the strategies I hope to implement to overcome it. From a practical perspective, it is important to let others know what I'm going through and my plans to bring the crisis to a desirable conclusion. My friends care about me; they want to know what is going on in my life, what my crisis management plans are, and what they can do to help. Caring for others is normal and expected Christian deportment. Thus, articulating, as appropriate with your close companions, is a humble thing to do so your friends can pray and assist you as you go through the crisis.

## The Hard Side

Discerning the second, not-so-obvious part of trials is imperative for the Christian, too. This part is less about crisis management and more about what your Lord is teaching you as He takes you through the crisis. Our unbelieving culture has only one story: they can tell you what they are going through and what they plan to do about it. Their story is myopic in that they have no other benchmark or example to emulate. They find the best hope in their strength, ability, plan, strategy, and fortitude. However, Christians intuitively know that God is not only in the background of their stories but also actively speaking, working, and engaging on their behalf. The Christian understands that the stories they are going through are more about drawing attention to God than the actual real time and space aspects of the crisis. The crisis is the Christian's opportunity to spread the fame of Jesus near and far. If the point of your life and marriage is more about God than yourself, as it should be, most assuredly, the hardships you go through are more about the glory the Father receives than the personal comfort or security you experience.

## What He Said

My old friend Job reminds me of a believer who went through some of life's most excruciating trials, but his faith, like a stained garment, bled through the pain he endured. Over the years, I have found inexpressible comfort in Job's trust in God. He was weak, tired, and, at times, bitter. He received little help from his friends, and even his wife could have been a better supporter. God was determined not to give Job explanations for his trials. And for Job, it did not have to make perfect sense. His faith was not resting in the hope of understanding the problem but in a good God who was able to do the impossible. Here is what he said:

> Then Job arose and tore his robe and shaved his head and fell on the ground and worshiped. And he said, "Naked I came from my mother's womb, and naked shall I return. The LORD gave, and the LORD has taken away; blessed be the name of the LORD."
> (Job 1:20-21)

## Time to Reflect

When the movie about your marriage ends, what will people remember: the problems in your marriage or the Scriptwriter who did great things through you and your marriage, even using the hardships to mature you and spread His fame?

## Practical Suggestion

Talk to your spouse about how God can be more glorified in your lives and marriage.

# 22

# Five Tips for Arguing

*What causes quarrels and fights among you? Is it not this, that your passions are at war within you? You desire and do not have, so you murder.*

(James 4:1-2)

It is impossible to live in a fallen world and not argue or disagree with another person. From birth to the grave, disagreements are part of life. The odds are so stacked against you that you will not be able to get through life without conflict, which is why it would be good to learn how to argue well, especially with your spouse. Here are five tips for your marriage communication.

**EXPECT THE OBVIOUS:** A right understanding of the doctrines of man and sin will bring your expectations down to a sensible level. There are no authentic, righteous people in the world today, not without Christ's alien righteousness. We all are sinners. No one has escaped Adam's curse. If you are surprised by your spouse's sin, you have forgotten the obvious: your spouse is not perfect. I am not making a case to sin more, and I'm not making light of sin, but I am stating the obvious: as John said, if you say you don't sin, you're a liar (1 John 1:7-10).

**BE SUSPICIOUS:** Humble biblical suspicion is essential when you are observing and sizing up others. Jesus said in Matthew 7:3-5 that if you perceive the log is in your eye, you are in the right place to engage another imperfect person. Self-deception or stubbornness will keep you from seeing that big log in your eye, which will keep you from responding to your marital strife correctly. A person who is humbly self-suspicious is a person who can see clearly.

**REMEMBER WHO YOU WERE:** You put Jesus on Adam's tree. Because of your sin, the Father executed His Son on the cross. Because of your sin, the Son willingly chose to die on that cross. Your crime against the Lord of the universe makes you the biggest sinner that you know. All of the things done to you do not compare to what you did to Sovereign God. Paul understood this, even at the end of his life, as he labeled himself the foremost sinner (1 Timothy 1:15-16).

**ASK QUESTIONS:** Do not enter into conflict by making statements. Ask questions. Be suspicious of your unique assumptions by realizing you're working with insufficient data. It will usually be better for you to ask more questions before stating your opinion. It's easy to have a high opinion of your views and your rightness, which can keep you from asking proper questions.

**LITTLE TO DIE OVER:** Think about your past arguments. How many were so important that they warranted you to sin against God and your spouse? I recall, as a child, getting into an argument with my four brothers over a Snickers Bar. We were a poor family, and on that day, we had only one candy bar. One brother measured the candy bar with a ruler and did not divide the five parts equally. An argument ensued, and harsh things were said. Sadly, many of our arguments have not evolved much beyond the trivialities of sharing a candy bar.

## Time to Reflect

Perhaps you are currently in a disagreement with your spouse. If so, based on the five tips, here are a few reflective questions:

1. **EXPECTATIONS:** Why are you surprised that your spouse does wrong?
2. **SUSPICIOUS:** Are you more suspicious of yourself than your spouse?
3. **REMEMBER:** Who is the foremost sinner in your marriage, from your perspective?
4. **QUESTIONS:** Do you typically believe you have all the facts when you talk with your spouse?
5. **TRIVIALITIES:** Is it more important for you to be right or restorative if right and restorative are at odds with each other?

## Practical Suggestion

James said you sinfully argue because you have warring idols inside you. As you reflect on the tips and questions in this devotion, how do you need to change to be a more effective and redemptive communicator?

# 23

# Bible Study Hurts Marriage

*However, let each one of you love his wife as himself,*
*and let the wife see that she respects her husband.*
*(Ephesians 5:33)*

Mable knocked on my counseling door. She was in tears. She had just finished her weekly women's Bible study. The deep dive into God's Word was exhilarating, and the fellowship with her friends was refreshing, but Mable was in tears. Quizzically, I could not connect her tears with her time with God and friends. It did not make sense to me. Then she asked, "Would you talk to my husband?" Seven syllables. It spoke volumes. Mable spent a few hours each Tuesday at their church building watching a video from a famous woman speaker on random Bible topics. At some point during these Bible studies, Mable started thinking that something was missing in her life. What she perceived as good—her Bible study—was becoming an unpleasant reminder of something unsatisfying about her marriage.

In a moment of clarity, she realized her Bible study and friends had subtly become her surrogate husband, mentor, friend, and confidant. Mable was not saying her Bible study was unbiblical—no, not at all. However, it was becoming clear to her that this fantastic weekly event had morphed into a sub-biblical context that caused her to forget about her husband's leadership role and the complementarian responsibilities that he has to help them pursue God together. Biff was not leading Mable spiritually, particularly in the most important way a man should serve his wife: in her pursuit of God. Though Mable had no plans or biblical mandate to stop her Bible study, the Lord was gently pressing her consciousness to change the spiritual dearth in their marriage.

Studying the Bible with friends is not wrong. Mable's problem was that the study of the Bible and its context, which was spurring her toward holiness, was happening within the context of her secondary relationships rather than her primary human relationship. She was benefiting from participating in the Bible study, but her good times with close friends highlighted her marital loneliness. Her spiritual maturation in secondary relationships exacerbated the dysfunction of her primary relationship. Thus, Mable stood in my office crying. The Bible clearly teaches that a husband should love his wife the way he loves himself and that the wife should respect her husband. These are not either/or callings but both/and.

- What better way can a man love his wife than by spiritually leading her?
- Why motivate her to pursue secondary relationships for primary care or make it difficult for her to respect her husband?

Seeking supplemental discipleship contexts is smart and wise, but nothing should replace matrimonial koinonia. Bible studies can complement a person's spiritual growth, just like a book, a blog, or a buddy. Still, the issue for Mable was not her supplemental contexts and relationships. Mable's problem was her husband's disconnect from what the Lord was doing in her life. Her struggle is similar to that of parents who delegate their children's spiritual guidance to the local church. Mable's friends were more intimate with and knowledgeable of her than Biff was. Mable had a clearly torn one-flesh union. Half of her one-flesh was spiritually alive, while the other part was spiritually disconnected and dying. If this were her physical body, she would be on her deathbed.

## Time to Reflect

Perhaps your go-to secondary relationship that refreshes your soul is not a Bible study with friends like it was for Mable. Your closest camaraderie might be with your buddies from work or your favorite social media platform. Maybe it's your children, a passionate hobby, or sports. Secondary relationships that make you feel better do not have to be wrong. They can be a mistake if they keep the husband from leading his wife and his wife from respecting her husband.

## Practical Suggestion

Is your spouse your best spiritual friend? If not, will you start asking God to change you and your spouse? Do not let anything tear away at your one-flesh union.

# 24

# Sex and Marriage

*It is good for a man not to have sexual relations with a woman. But because of the temptation to sexual immorality, each man should have his own wife and each woman her own husband.*

*(1 Corinthians 7:1-2)*

Physical intimacy with your spouse requires more from each spouse. Physical intimacy demands more from the couple. You can do many things as a married couple and even pretend to get along, but sex is the litmus test that tells the truth about the marriage. It is not unusual for a couple to attend church together for 30 years and be miserable in their marriage. Though they can pretend in the public domain, they cannot be fake in the privacy of their bedroom. Intimacy is either right, and your marriage is good, or it is not, and your marriage is in trouble. If your sexual life is struggling, it is because of sin. Sin separates, and the bedroom is the most prominent place where you will perceive this division. If you do not deal with sin biblically, the tectonic plates of your sex life will shift, and your marriage will be off-kilter. No matter what you do, you will be out of harmony with each other.

*Then the eyes of both were opened, and they knew that they were naked. And they sewed fig leaves together and made themselves loincloths.*
*(Genesis 3:7)*

Sin is what happened to our first sexual couple. Sin entered the picture, and it divided Adam and Eve by shame, guilt, and fear, which prompted them to hide, blame, and run (Genesis 3:7). This one verse explains eloquently, powerfully, and sadly why sex can be such a problem in marriage and why it is an indicator of the deeper problems a couple can experience. When sin enters, the fig leaves come on, people start hiding from each other, and the desire for vulnerability, exposure, openness, honesty, and transparency vanish. You cannot have biblical physical intimacy while wearing fig leaves. Suppose there is unresolved bitterness, anger, frustration, guilt, disrespect, unforgiveness, hurt, malice, or insensitivity in your marriage. In that case, you will be hesitant to become completely vulnerable in physical intimacy with your spouse.

No doubt a man can be mean to his wife and demand sex from her. I am also aware a woman can despise her husband and still have sex with him. Hate or disrespect toward each other and having sex is not biblical sex. Biblical sex is an uninhibited willingness to unite with another person in God-centered, other-centered unity physically. God-centered sex is the most intimate picture of Christ and His church—fully and comprehensively united as husband and wife (Ephesians 5:28-30). A poor sexual relationship is a symptom, not a cause. Though the symptom is inside the bedroom, the cause is outside, specifically in the hearts of the couple. If you do not fix the cause, your sexual experience with your spouse will never be right. Let me illustrate: Suppose Biff slapped Mable across the face at 5 PM. It is now 10 PM, and Biff wants to have sex. Do you think Mable can freely give herself to Biff? Though you may have never slapped your spouse, you may have done things that have caused your spouse to put layers on, which has restricted your sexual experience.

## Time to Reflect

1.  When you think about physical intimacy with your spouse, what is the first thing that comes to your mind?
2.  Are you free to be vulnerable with your spouse during physical intimacy? If not, what impedes your mutual transparent relationship?
3.  Are there things that you brought into your marriage that inhibit you from being sexually free with your spouse? What are those things?
4.  Are there unresolved issues in your marriage that keep you from uninhibited physical intimacy? What are those things?

## Practical Suggestion

Share your reflective thoughts with your spouse. If you cannot share these things with your spouse, please find a competent mentor friend of the same gender to get their perspective and care. As you share with your mentor, ask the Father to give you the freedom and opportunity to start sharing these things with your spouse. The ultimate goal of this devotional is to talk about these matters with your spouse freely.

# 25

# The Double Confession

*Therefore, confess your sins to one another and pray for one another, that you may be healed.*

(James 5:16)

Biff sinned against Mable, and Mable was hurt. Biff asked Mable to forgive him. Mable forgave Biff. They reconciled—but not really. Though Mable forgave Biff, she neglected to tell him that she was sinning against him because of what he had done to her. Though she understood that it is never right to sin in response to being sinned against, she did sin against Biff as a response to his sin.

- Have you ever responded sinfully to your spouse who sinned against you?
- Did you confess your sin against your spouse who sinned against you?

A double confession is when the one who sinned asks for forgiveness, and the offended also asks for forgiveness, recognizing they sinned in response to the offender's sin. Because of fallenness, double sinning happens more often than you might think. A husband, for example, can be harsh or unkind toward his wife. God brings conviction, and he repents. But rather than working through all the ramifications of his sin, the wife harbors sinful anger toward him. He confesses, but she does not. There is no one-flesh reconciliation because of the unperceived, unmentioned, and unresolved fracture in their marriage. It is unwise to dismiss, justify, or ignore any sin in your one-flesh union, even if you were the offended one.

Sin is sin regardless of who does it, and there is only one right response to its encroachments: confess, forgive, reconcile. A well-loved wife lets her husband know about her sin and seeks his forgiveness. These attitudes and actions reconcile them, which releases them to enjoy the unencumbered fullness of what a one-flesh union should be. Perhaps someone would say, "Sounds great, but what if your husband is immature?" Many wives have shared how their husbands are brutish or insensitive; they don't have the liberty to have this kind of dialogue with their husbands because of their sulking or retaliations. What these wives are admitting is a legitimate fear. If the husband and wife are not on the same confessional page—confessing to and forgiving each other regularly— the stubborn spouse will inhibit the willing spouse from being transparent, which is why every home should be a context of grace that permits the drawing out of and speaking into each others' lives.

- **CREATE GRACE CONTEXTS:** Release your spouse from fear of you by creating a context of grace in your home. Encourage and invite your spouse to bring critique into your life. Make it easy for them to serve you in your sanctification. After they bring critique, support them and express your gratitude for their corrective care. Your spouse married you because they love you. Respect your spouse enough to let them help you with your deficiencies (Genesis 2:18).

- **CAREFULLY DRAW OUT:** As you perceive your spouse's sin in response to yours, humbly come alongside them with insightful questions. Never forget that the log in your eye is so much larger than the speck you are examining (Matthew 7:3-5). The context of grace you have created will release them to respond to your redemptive questions.

For the first five years of our marriage, I never confessed any sin to my wife. Remarkably, it did not occur to me that my lack of confession was tearing away at our marriage. As God began to dismantle my self-righteousness and self-reliance, I began to clearly see how I was a habituated "sweep it under the rug" guy. My first confession was to God. My second was to my wife. Then, it was time to create an environment of grace, which began by looking under the rug.

## Time to Reflect

1. Do you sin in response to your spouse's sin?
2. Are you aware that harboring unconfessed sin can turn into bitterness and other forms of anger?
3. What needs to happen for you and your spouse to become habituated double-confessors?

## Practical Suggestion

Talk to your spouse about the importance of an environment of grace in your home and how you both can work together to make it a place where everyone is free to confess their sins to each other.

# 26

# The Marriage Won't Change

But we preach Christ crucified, a stumbling block to Jews and folly to Gentiles, but to those who are called, both Jews and Greeks, Christ the power of God and the wisdom of God. For the foolishness of God is wiser than men, and the weakness of God is stronger than men.

(1 Corinthians 1:23-25)

**WARNING:**
*This devotion is not for a spouse in an abusive marriage. If your marriage is abusive, find help immediately to stop the abuse.*

It is important to accurately recognize how God is working in you during times of suffering. Many times, individuals see their trials as something that is happening to them rather than something that God is doing in them. Acknowledging that God is doing something in you is more than a courtesy nod. It is sobering. For God to take an interest in helping any of us is both humbling and frightening (See Job 23:15).

## Ask the Good Question

Many times, in suffering, it's easy to focus on the wrong question. We can be more concerned about whether God is safe than whether He is good. Sometimes, our genuine desire and expectation for self-protection can overpower the Lord's good work in our lives (Romans 8:28). The cross of Christ is the most profound testimony of the safe/good dynamic. The Jews saw the cross as a stumbling block, while the Greeks saw it as foolishness. From God's perspective, the cross was wisdom and power. There are times in your life when what is best for you is not necessarily the safest path for you. In those moments, you must understand and believe that God is good and He is working good in you. Like the baker kneading the dough, your great God is working His transcendent purposes into you by making you a vessel fit for His aims (2 Corinthians 4:7).

## Crucible of Suffering

While in the crucible of suffering, remember to make copious mental notes of what He is doing in you. Do not forget the pain. Embrace the suffering. By embracing the agony, you are embracing the God who is working the agony into your life. Though Christ wanted His Father to take away the cup, He ultimately embraced the Father's work in His life when He said, "Not my will, but Your will be done" (See Luke 22:42). Jesus submitted to His Father, even though it meant He would die. He believed in the good purposes of the Father (Hebrews 12:2). When you stop resisting your Father's work in your life and start believing in Him, there is hope for change in you.

However, to accept the crucible of suffering does not mean your adversity will pass. It only means you are going to trust the steady hand of God, who is working for your good, regardless of the consequences. Believing in God does not mean things will turn out the way you had hoped.

- Christ embraced the will of the Father, which led to His crucifixion.
- Joseph embraced God's will, and his life involved disappointment after disappointment.
- Job said, "Though He slay me, I will hope in Him" ( Job 13:15).
- Paul believed in God and was beheaded.
- Peter followed his Savior to his crucifixion.

Believing in God during your time of adversity is a desire to know and follow God regardless of where the path may lead. But you can be assured of this one thing: God is good. Though you may not know the outcome of His good work in your life, rest assured that you will be more than satisfied by relinquishing your rights to Him.

## Time to Reflect

1. What are you learning about yourself through your marital challenges?
2. What are you learning about God?
3. How is what you're learning maturing you?

## Practical Suggestion

If you are not able to talk to your spouse about these things, find someone of the same gender who is willing to walk with you during your time in the crucible. You may share this devotion with them. Perhaps it will encourage them or recalibrate their marriage.

# 27

# Suffering Produces Strength

*Not only that, but we rejoice in our sufferings, knowing that suffering produces endurance, and endurance produces character, and character produces hope, and hope does not put us to shame, because God's love has been poured into our hearts through the Holy Spirit who has been given to us.*

(Romans 5:3-5)

Discomfort in life is as assured as death and taxes. There are some things you can count on, and personal suffering is one of them. It is part of the package that comes with the gift of a new life from God (Philippians 1:29). Because suffering is guaranteed, it's important to give reflective thoughts on how you respond when you don't get your way. What comes out of your mouth when you do not get your way reveals your theology of suffering, your theology of God, and your maturity as a Christian. Jesus was correct when He said that out of the abundance of the heart, the mouth speaks (Luke 6:45). Even though you cannot see your heart, you can discern your heart by what comes out of your mouth, and nothing will give you more clarity about your heart than those moments when you do not get your way. During seasons of personal comfort, you can manage your words because there are no challenges to your desires, whether those desires are for good or evil. It is during times when you do not get your way that your practical theology will manifest (Read Romans 5:3-5). Paul taught that our faith gives us access to the grace of God, and through that grace, we stand. The progression goes like this:

1.  **GRANTING:** God gives you the gift of faith—salvation.
2.  **ACCESSING:** Because of the faith given, you have access to God's grace.
3.  **ENABLING:** It is God's grace that allows you to interact with personal suffering.
4.  **PRODUCING:** Personal suffering produces endurance, character, and hope.

How are you living in the grace that God provides you? You can discern the answer by how you respond to your suffering. Difficulties do not necessarily have a purpose in themselves. Suffering is suffering. Everybody suffers. Even the unregenerate world suffers. They become sick and die. They are in traffic accidents. They divorce just like the Christian community. The difference between the unregenerate person who suffers and the believer who suffers is God. Though our lost friends experience the realities of suffering, none of them find faith, grace, endurance, character, or hope. Christians are the only ones who can experience God through suffering because they have a relationship with Him, and they understand that He is working in their suffering.

It is God who is producing Christ in your life through your suffering. Suffering does not produce godlike character qualities. If that were true, the lost person would mature through suffering like a Christian. It is God working through your adversity, bringing out His good purposes in your life.

You must choose whether to fixate on your problems or center your thoughts on God, who is seeking to form Christ in you through the problems you are experiencing. The words you choose to discuss your problems will provide the information you need to understand how your heart is aligned with God's will in you. The God-centered heart produces God-centered language according to the model that Paul lays out in Romans 5:3-5. This kind of person talks about his problems as one who is enduring through his problems—a person who is fortified even though suffering persists. You can understand the character of Christ by the fruit of the Spirit, which will be evident to others through your speech patterns (Galatians 5:22-23).

## Time to Reflect

When you talk about your problems, what do you sound like most of the time: problem-centered or God-centered? Do you know the difference?

## Practical Suggestion

Will you speak with a friend about your reflections on this devotion? Invite their input. Also, ask the Lord to reveal to you each time you grumble this week. When the kind Spirit of God reveals those moments, repent immediately by confessing, seeking forgiveness, and making a plan to put the grumbling off, renew your mind, and put on Christlike behaviors.

# 28

# God Is There Before You

*All the descendants of Jacob were seventy persons; Joseph was already in Egypt.*

(Exodus 1:5)

You may not know where your marriage is leading you, but there is one thing I want you to know: Regardless of your journey, you can rest assured that God is well ahead of you and has made many preparations before you arrive. Like a great friend waiting to receive you at the end of a long journey, the good Lord is always ahead of you and has a well-prepared end in mind. In Exodus, God disrupts an entire nation. The Lord lets the Israelites know that the times are changing. There is turmoil in their land, and they are in dire straits. The famine has spread beyond discomfort, and their families are struggling to make ends meet. From their perspective, they were living in the moment, and there was little hope for change that would improve their future. It was not clear to them what they should do to resolve their problems. From their ground-level view, they had no idea of the plans that God had made for them in Egypt. In Exodus 1:5, the writer tells us that the Israelites were leaving their homes and heading to an unknown place in Egypt. Though the text does not say, I'm sure some of them were struggling with the stirring of their nests (Deuteronomy 32:11). God created an uncomfortable situation because He was writing a story that was far beyond anything they could think or imagine (Ephesians 3:20).

- What was a time or two in your marriage when you distinctly felt that God was changing your circumstances for reasons you could not understand?
- From your ground-level perspective, were you confident that God had a good plan for both of you?

It was time for a lifestyle change. New people, places, and things were the new normal for the Israelites, and there wasn't a thing they could do about it. And then, the writer inserted five little words into the Bible: "Joseph was already in Egypt." Think for a moment what it meant for Joseph to be already in Egypt, waiting to receive his dysfunctional family and confused friends. It took the mighty hand of God to rip Joseph away from his family so that the Lord could reposition him in Egypt. God also used a few Ishmaelite tradesmen, an evil woman, some jail time, and Pharaoh's favor. To miss "Joseph was already in Egypt" misses the profundity of what God did by a zillion miles. Joseph's story is more mind-bending than just prepping a place for a few friends and family. God went to great lengths to get Joseph to Egypt because that is what God does for those He loves. God is always persevering with you. He is always planning and working ahead of time, so when you arrive, you'll be amazed that God is already there. Whether it's Joseph's family turmoil or your marriage problems, what you are experiencing on the ground level is not the same as what God is doing on the sovereign level. The Lord works in interfamily disputes in such a way that you will never be able to figure it out until He lets you know, and when you do find out, it will blow your mind.

## Time to Reflect

1. When you look at your marriage problems from the ground level, what do you see? How does it feel? What are you experiencing?
2. When you think about your Father planning, removing, repositioning, and inserting things into your marriage, does it bring more hope than fear? Please explain.

## Practical Suggestion

Take some time to read chapters 37-50 of Genesis while keeping Exodus 1:5 in mind. Ask the Father to calm your soul as you watch Him work, knowing that no matter where He takes your marriage, He will be waiting when you arrive.

# 29

# Ten Ways to Ignore Problems

*For when I kept silent, my bones wasted away through my groaning all day long. For day and night your hand was heavy upon me; my strength was dried up as by the heat of summer.*

(Psalm 32:3-4)

Resist sin in your marriage at every turn. Do not think that you are the exception or that you are somehow above sin, and it will not destroy you. When you see it, kill it. If it is more than you can handle, call for the caregivers (local church) and let them help you kill it. The most ungracious thing you can do is let it persist in your marriage. I've counseled many spouses who refused to take this advice. Instead of implementing a biblical plan to restore the brokenness in their marriages, they nourished and cherished other things that became replacements for their infected marriages. Here are ten of those marriage replacements:

1. **MINISTRY:** Serving others is a common marriage replacement. Whether a pastor or someone else serving in a similar role, their ministry became

their new marriage partner. The marriage-to-ministry problem is bigger than you might imagine. A lot of praise can come through the door of ministry, which can be satisfying for a person in a dissatisfying marriage.

2.  **WORK:** A person's vocation is similar to the ministry replacement. It's a place for a spouse to get their approval fix. Their marriage is unfulfilling, so they put all their energy, skill, and time into their job. They use the job card as the de facto answer to why they do not devote more time to the family. "I work all day" is the excuse, which can be a smoke screen to justify their dissatisfaction with their spouse.

3.  **CHILDREN:** A spouse in an unsatisfactory marriage may find an outlet through their children. Rather than enjoying their spouse, they move their primary human affection to their children. It is not unusual for the child-centered or workaholic parent to divorce after 35 years of marriage. After they retire and the kids are gone, the distractions are also gone.

4.  **FLIRTING:** Husbands and wives may resort to flirting in the workplace or the church to satisfy their cravings for soul-to-soul companionship.

5.  **PORN:** Many spouses enjoy the private fantasy world of porn as a spousal replacement. Through the Internet, they construct their fantastical mental narratives. The cyber actors virtually adore the spouse as they enjoy a temporary break from a unfulfilling marriage.

6.  **FRIENDS:** Spouses are particularly susceptible to the best friend trap, especially their friends who want spiritual intimacy or nonjudgmental companionship. Bible studies and sports bars can become surrogate spouses for those longing for emotional bonding.

7. **SOCIAL MEDIA:** The most popular free therapy outlet is the Internet. It's a person's favorite social media site where they spend an excessive amount of time scrolling.

8. **APPROVAL:** At the root of all brokenness in marriages lurks the desire to be appreciated by someone. If the wife is demanding or a nag or the husband is inattentive or harsh, the hurt spouse is tempted to look for any means to find someone who approves and appreciates them.

9. **STRENGTHS:** A person's strength is their greatest weakness, especially if they are using their skills and abilities to fill their cravings while ignoring their marriage.

10. **DISTORT THE TRUTH:** If your marriage is not what it should be and you don't find help to resolve the problems, you will be tempted to alter God's Word to rationalize your life and marriage. Perhaps you blame your spouse or justify your anger. Sin unchecked, like cancer, will cause more problems.

## Time to Reflect

1. As you read the list, which ones most closely align with your marriage?

2. What would you add to the list that most closely reflects your marriage replacement temptations?

## Practical Suggestion

If your marriage is dissatisfying, do not ignore or justify your marriage replacements. Ask God to help you identify what is happening and make a plan to remove what is wrong from your life.

# 30

# I Lead You; I Sin Against You

*When Jesus had received the sour wine, he said, "It is finished," and he bowed his head and gave up his spirit.*

(John 19:30)

Biff does not want to lead his wife. He feels like a hypocrite trying to lead her while sporadically sinning against her. Biff asked his counselor, "How can I lead her and sin against her at the same time?" Admittedly, Mable does not make it any easier on Biff as she reminds him of his sin when he tries to lead her. Biff took the position that it is better not to lead Mable at all if he's going to sin against her. He has three options.

## Three Options

- He will not lead his wife until he reaches a state of sinless perfection.
- He will not lead his wife but continues sinning against her.
- He leads his wife while recognizing he's an imperfect leader. Biff acknowledges that he is a sinner called to lead his wife.

Currently, neither Biff nor Mable has an accurate or clear understanding of the gospel—at least as it applies to this situation. The Bible informs us that we are sinners in need of a Savior. God's Word reveals that there will never be a day in our lives when we will not be tempted to sin, and on some days, we will succumb to those temptations. Because your spouse is the closest individual to you, it stands to reason that you will sin against your spouse more than anyone else. Both partners must humbly understand and apply these two practical truths:

- God calls a husband to lead his wife.
- The husband will sin against his wife.

Mable believes Biff is getting off the hook too easily by genuinely confessing his sin and asking for forgiveness. What she does not perceive is the expensiveness of the gospel. The death of Christ on the cross and His eventual resurrection from the grave was an infinite payment for an infinite crime against an infinite Being. To suggest that Biff should pay more than an infinite price for his sin is untenable, plus a mockery of the gospel. Biff is also mocking the gospel by refusing to lead his wife while justifying his passivity by acknowledging he is a sinner. He must accept that he is a saint and a sinner, and sinning is something saints do. Biff needs to get over himself while simultaneously flinging himself on the only person who can clean up his sporadic messes.

He needs to appropriate God's grace in his life each time he sins and live in the riches and freedom of that gospel experience. Ironically, he confesses his sin against his wife while picking up a host of other sins, such as self-pity, regret, shame, and guilt—all clear indicators that the gospel is not enough for Biff. His gospel is anemic, and Mable is living out her form of gospel dysfunction by not letting Biff off the hook. She agrees with Biff: he must pay for his sin, and though the cross of Christ is a good start, there must be more. While not minimizing any sin against anyone, Mable is missing a vital point of the gospel: Christ died for sins. She has unwittingly put herself in God's role. Mable is the sole determiner and executioner of the fair judgment of her husband's sins. Ironically, she does not hold others to this anti-gospel standard: Christ's death is sufficient for her friends and even her enemies, but she has a Christ-plus penalty box when it comes to Biff.

## Time to Reflect

Will you spend time over the next few days thinking about these two statements? Perhaps sharing them with a friend, in the context of this devotion, will aid in your reflections.

1. Does your theology say, "God's Judgment of His Son + Your Judgment of Your Spouse = Satisfied Debt?"
2. Does "God's Judgment of His Son + Nothing = Satisfied Debt," which releases you from punishing your spouse when they sin?

## Practical Suggestion

How do you need to change to bring your life and marriage in line with the gospel? Start changing with a prayer to your Father now. Afterward, make a practical plan to avoid the anemic gospel trap.

# 31

# Ask This Question Daily

*You shall love the Lord your God with all your heart and with all your soul and with all your strength and with all your mind, and your neighbor as yourself.*
(Luke 10:27)

Your spouse is two parts—body and soul. Every person is a dichotomy—organic and nonorganic or physical and spiritual. Though the two parts interrelate and affect each other, there are distinctions between them, which require different care. The word body is a basket word that includes all the parts of the body, like your hair, skin, lungs, heart, blood, and toenails. Healthy body parts work together to permit you to function at optimal levels. Though each body part is interrelated, each one is independent and needs a particular kind of care. The independence of the parts is why you want to be specific when trying to help a person who is hurting. For example, if a person has a tummy ache, you don't ask them about their ankles. They might say, "My ankles are fine; it's my stomach that is killing me." You cared for them but asked the wrong question. Asking the right question is essential. A doctor asks a general question rather than a specific one, "How are you doing today?" He asks you a non-specific question that allows you to answer it in a specific way.

Likewise, your soul is similar to your body. It's a basket word that houses all the soul parts, such as the heart, spirit, mind, thoughts, imagination, intentions, will, dreams, emotions, conscience, attitudes, faith, confidence, hope, fears, and more. Because I am not God, I do not know the thoughts and intentions of my wife's heart (Hebrews 4:12-13), which is why the question that I ask her more than any other is, "How is your soul today?" It is a general, non-specific question. It is rare for a day to go by when I'm not asking her that question. Rather than thinking that I know what is going on inside of her or, even worse, telling her what is going on inside of her, I ask her. Similar to a medical doctor, I intentionally leave the question open-ended and non-specific. I want her to fill in the blank by getting specific with my generalized question.

Perhaps she fears today. I need to know that so I can serve her with practical soul care. With the soul question, she has the liberty to answer it accurately and without my assumptions. If she is afraid, she may say, "I'm struggling with taking my thoughts captive today," which is something she has said in the past. Her response is my call to action to help her connect the dots with possible other soul parts that may relate to and feed her fears, such as thoughts, dreams, imagination, attitude, conscience, and even sleep deprivation, which is the physical dimension that impacts the spiritual. When one part is struggling, it will always affect other parts, too. This concept is the same for the body and soul. By serving your spouse this way, you are not only helping yourself—because you are one—but you are helping your spouse avert potential physical issues that can come to the surface as they bubble up from the soul.

For example, a friend of ours was struggling with physical pain in her jaw. She was grinding her teeth while sleeping. My wife asked her about a decision their family was making and how her self-confessed worry, anxiety, and fear might be causing the physical pain. The lady agreed. She decided she would not discuss this family decision before bedtime but only during the day. Her jaw relaxed, and the physical problem disappeared. The soul and the body are interrelated. Perhaps you want to ask the question the way your doctor does: "How are you doing today?" That's fine as long as you both know the intent of the question and your spouse has the freedom to answer according to what's happening in their soul.

## Time to Reflect

1. How well do you do soul care with your spouse?
2. What does soul care look like on a day-to-day basis?
3. Do you spend more time caring for the body than the soul?
4. How is your soul today?
5. How is your spouse's soul today?

## Practical Suggestion

Think about how you can be a better soul care physician with your spouse and enact your plan. Talk about the wisdom of an open-ended question where you both have the liberty to explain what is going on exactly.

## About the Author

 Rick Thomas launched the Life Over Coffee global training network in 2008 to bring hope and help for you and others by creating resources that spark conversations for transformation. His primary responsibilities are resource creation and leadership development, which he does through speaking, writing, podcasting, and educating. In 1990 he earned a BA in Theology and, in 1991, a BS in Education. In 1993, he received his ordination into Christian ministry, and in 2000, he graduated with an MA in Counseling from The Master's University. In 2006, he was recognized as a Fellow of the Association of Certified Biblical Counselors (ACBC).

## Other Books Available from Life Over Coffee

Boasting in Weakness
Centering Your Marriage on Christ
Communication
Complete Marriage
Don't Apologize
Exchange the Truth for a Lie
Help My Marriage Has Grown Cold
Identity Crisis
Local Church
Loving Me
Mad
Marriage Devotion We Are One
Politics and Culture
Parenting Devotion from Zero to Adulthood
Sex, Temptation, and Modesty
Storm Hurler
The Cyber Effect
The Talk
Wives Leading
You Decide

www.ingramcontent.com/pod-product-compliance
Lightning Source LLC
Chambersburg PA
CBHW071514120626
46550CB00006B/2223